IT'S TIME TO EAT SWISS CHARD

It's Time to Eat SWISS CHARD

Walter the Educator

Silent King Books
A WhichHead Entertainment Imprint

Copyright © 2025 by Walter the Educator

All rights reserved. No part of this book may be reproduced in any manner whatsoever without written per- mission except in the case of brief quotations embodied in critical articles and reviews.

First Printing, 2024

Disclaimer

This book is a literary work; the story is not about specific persons, locations, situations, and/or circumstances unless mentioned in a historical context. Any resemblance to real persons, locations, situations, and/or circumstances is coincidental. This book is for entertainment and informational purposes only. The author and publisher offer this information without warranties expressed or implied. No matter the grounds, neither the author nor the publisher will be accountable for any losses, injuries, or other damages caused by the reader's use of this book. The use of this book acknowledges an understanding and acceptance of this disclaimer.

It's Time to Eat SWISS CHARD is a collectible early learning book by Walter the Educator suitable for all ages belonging to Walter the Educator's Time to Eat Book Series. Collect more books at WaltertheEducator.com

USE THE EXTRA SPACE TO TAKE NOTES AND DOCUMENT YOUR MEMORIES

SWISS CHARD

It's time to eat, come gather near,

It's Time to Eat
Swiss Chard

A special treat is growing here!

With leaves so green and stems so bright,

Swiss chard is such a lovely sight!

It stretches tall in garden beds,

With colors bright, yellows, reds!

Some stems are pink, some orange too,

A rainbow just for me and you!

The leaves are big and soft to touch,

They curl and crinkle, oh so much!

They shimmer in the morning light,

A leafy green that's pure delight!

We pick some chard and wash it well,

A splash of water, can you tell?

The dirt is gone, it's clean and bright,

Now it's ready, what a sight!

We chop it up, so nice and small,

Into a pan, we drop it all.

A little sizzle, hear that sound?

The chard is cooking, swirling 'round!

It smells so fresh, it smells so sweet,

It's Time to Eat
Swiss Chard

A tasty dish that's fun to eat!

With just a pinch of salt to add,

It's simple food that makes us glad!

We take a bite, so soft, so mild,

It's good for every grown-up, child!

Full of goodness, strong and bright,

It helps us run and play just right!

Eat it plain or in a stew,

With eggs, with rice, so much to do!

Swiss chard is yummy, don't you see?

A super snack for you and me!

So when you see those colors shine,

Remember, chard is fresh and fine!

Pick some up and cook with care,

A garden treat for all to share!

It's Time to Eat
Swiss Chard

Now we're full and feeling great,

Swiss chard makes a perfect plate!

Healthy, tasty, fun to chew,

It's Time to Eat
Swiss Chard

Try some chard, it's good for you!

ABOUT THE CREATOR

Walter the Educator is one of the pseudonyms for Walter Anderson. Formally educated in Chemistry, Business, and Education, he is an educator, an author, a diverse entrepreneur, and he is the son of a disabled war veteran.
"Walter the Educator" shares his time between educating and creating. He holds interests and owns several creative projects that entertain, enlighten, enhance, and educate, hoping to inspire and motivate you. Follow, find new works, and stay up to date with Walter the Educator™

at WaltertheEducator.com

www.ingramcontent.com/pod-product-compliance
Lightning Source LLC
LaVergne TN
LVHW052016060526
838201LV00059B/4043